When Life Gives You Lemons

Dealing with the Bitterness of Life

By

LeTasha S. Robinson

Foreword By

Evangelist Termeka Jacobs

When Life Gives You Lemons
Dealing with the Bitterness of Life
ISBN 978-0-615-98320-2
Copyright © 2015 by
LeTasha S. Robinson
PO Box 15
Lexington, South Carolina, 29071

Dedication and Thanks

This book is dedicated to the man that has been consistent in my life. He has never left me nor forsaken me. He is my friend, my father, and my leader; my Heavenly Father. I love this man more and more with each passing day. He has inspired and encouraged me to finish this book. I give him all praise and honor for without him there would be no me.

To both my natural and spiritual family I so appreciate how you have assisted me with my growth. To the greatest church on this side of Heaven (in my opinion) Zion Hopewell under the leadership of Bishop and Elder White. How you have held my hand and comforted me during many times on this journey. I am a Zionite! My mom and dad the Seibles I luv you more! I thank God for you all and pray that He bless you tremendously.

To the editors of the book Joylynn Ross (E.N. Joy) and Ada Rosario thank you all for your help. I started off reading your work J. Ross you then became a mentor and now my editor thank you for your assistance with making my thoughts into a story.

To JB and his family I love, love, love you all and thank for taking me in and just loving on me.

Finally, this book is dedicated to those who felt like life was unfair. May God grant you the peace in every situation that is trying to make you bitter and may His love fill every bitter area in your life.

Foreword

Have you ever wondered why thoughts, emotions and feelings return to you after having tried everything to rid of them? You have tried praying about it, fasting, talking it out, fighting or even ignoring it. Here's a thought: there may be something deeper.

In search to find out where her road began, LeTasha Robinson found out that there was something deeper to what she had experienced. She discovered that underneath the surface of depression, anger, frustration, unforgiveness and a slew of unanswered questions, there was a root called "bitterness." Negative emotions have the ability to resurface unless they are cut from the root. When I think of this dynamic author, I am reminded of II Corinthians 4:7-9" But we have this treasure in earthen vessels that the Excellency of the power may be of God, and not of us. We are troubled on every side, yet not distressed; we are perplexed, but not in despair; Persecuted, but not forsaken; cast down, but not destroyed."

Bitterness does not manifest overnight. Usually, the saying is that people "grow to be bitter." Just like a tree, the root is not visible above the surface, but it grows downward underneath the surface. What is visible, are the branches and the fruit or flowers that produce. Many times, negative feelings and emotions that are not dealt with reproduce. Adam and Eve disobeyed God, which birthed so many other things like: guilt, fear, shame, blame, rejection and displacement. Instead of being able to be in the blessings of God, they lived under a curse. This held true for every person that came after them. Basically, every problem that we face in life has a root cause to it. It is God's will for us to live freely and eternally. It is His good and perfect will that we live on purpose with His anointing to carry out His will in the earth. It is not His will for us to walk in bondage or be blinded by our sins. For this fact, He set a plan of redemption through Jesus Christ that we might be free again. Unfortunately, life challenges come our way and they may seem impossible to overcome them. When our plans seem to fail, when we get rejected by those whom we place value on, when become angry and frustrated, instead of saying, "this is only a test." As believers, we should always go back to our source, the Almighty God! What does He say about me? What does He say about my situation? What is the message behind all of this? Many times we go through life trying to make sense out of everything that happens to us. Instead, we should consider that God is trying to accomplish something through us. "Trust in the Lord with all thine heart; and lean not unto thine own understanding. In all thy ways acknowledge him, and he shall direct thy paths." (Proverbs 3:5-6) This is an easy scripture to quote, yet a trying scripture to live out. It becomes a challenge in itself, when all you feel is the pain, when all you see is opposition, when all you hear is rejection and your destined place seems so far away. You cry out for release, but it seems all you get is more situations that weigh you down. Trust in God will always lead us in the right direction, but when we try to figure things out on our own is when we run into issues.

When we taste something bitter, it is a sudden shock to our physical being. Immediately, we try to make it better by adding another ingredient to make it sweeter. We may even leave the item alone and spend time trying to get that awful taste out of our mouths. I can pretty much remember every bitter taste in my life: nasty medicine, sour orange, sour relationships, and terrible vacations. Bitter experiences cause us to avoid revisiting them. You may never want to travel to a place where you had a bad time. You may hesitate to get into another relationship. You may even stop eating certain foods because it left a bad taste in your mouth. No matter what span of time the hurt or discomfort took place, we seem to be able to remember it, as if it just happened. Sickness may come, feelings of depression may come, weariness may come, but where is it coming from? Better yet, what is feeding it? We can almost always trace these feelings back to some life-changing event. If we never get to the root of it, we will never truly become free from its grip. We will continue to circle around on life's runway, but never really take off. I believe God wants us healed and He wants us whole. He wants us to be able to live the life that He intended for all of His children. John 10:10 says, "The thief cometh not, but for to steal, and to kill, and to destroy: I am come that they might have life, and that they might have it more abundantly." In order for us to partake in this abundant life, we are going to have to know what needs to be uprooted and what needs to be grounded.

This book will have you inspired in the midst of your most trying times. The revelation of a story, which most people could not recover from or even survive through, is simply amazing. You will see how God gave this awesome Woman of God a strategy and a business out of her pain. "When Life Gives You Lemons" is more than a great read; it is an encouragement to press forward through real life issues. It will show you how to transition from being "bitter" to "better". How God will take a situation that you thought would have taken you out and give you a testimony of healing and freedom. I am excited to know that as you read this book, you will choose the outcome of your situation, no matter how it began.

Termeka L. Jacobs
Evangelist
Zion Hopewell Full Gospel Family Worship Center

Table of Contents

Dedication

Foreword

Introduction

Introduction

Have you ever just wished that things would go your way? Have you ever felt like the world was against you and that no one was for you? Life can be bitter at times and can cause you to want to walk away from everything. It can have you believing that the world would be a better place without you.

What happens when life throws you one bitter curve-ball after another? What happens when it seems as though you are not entitled to the *happily ever after* that is at the end of the fairytales? Do you give up on everything? Do you simply sign off on the paperwork that this is just how you are supposed to be; unlucky in life?

I started writing this book in a freeness that I had never experienced before. I no longer felt compelled to walk with my head down because of a hidden fear of shame that had plagued my life for so many years. I felt free and it was so awkward for me to express to people how I felt. I no longer had the inner part of me that wanted to be angry at the world and mad at individuals who technically hadn't done anything to me. But because of a deep root of bitterness and rejection, in my mind, everyone was against me. Does this sound familiar?

One thing you can count on is that everyone will one day leave this earth, but it is the moments that are between your birth and your death that will be your legacy. So what is your life saying about you right now? Is it sad, lonely and bitter? Do you find yourself always looking at life for the negatives and never the positives? Do you think you are in a one man war with no one to lean on? If you fall into any of these categories, then this book is for you. It is for the one who has said, "Life has been bitter and I can find no sweetness in it." But after reading this book, my prayer is that that will no longer be your testimony.

On April 9, 1981 a visit was held between Ms. ▮ and Letasha. This was the first visit held since Letasha was placed in care. From April to July of that year, four more visits were scheduled but two were cancelled by Ms. ▮

Chapter One: Unwanted

Step One: Gathering all the Ingredients

When making lemonade the main ingredient is lemons. You have to squeeze the juice out of the lemons. The size of the container you will need to store the lemonade is determined by how much juice you will be producing. For this recipe we will be making a gallon of lemonade. So three to four large lemons or five to six small lemons will suffice. You will also need water, and sugar.

When I was younger no one could pay me to want to eat a lemon. They were bitter and tasted sour to me. I only wanted the things that were sweet, such as bananas, cakes, cookies and ice cream. Who would want to eat something bitter on purpose? Lemons were an unwanted fruit for me and I never could find its purpose until I learned how to make lemonade. Lemons have a purpose on earth even when I thought that they didn't. I never understood how lemons would fit into my world. But now they are a huge part of my life and I find myself searching out this fruit even more.

Living in a society where an eye for an eye is not frowned upon, we find more and more people angry and wanting to operate out of that anger. Anger can be a deadly weapon if not disposed of correctly. But how can it be disposed of correctly? I am not talking about killing, fighting, or doing any bodily harm. I'm talking about letting anger go and being free of it permanently. Is it really as easy as one, two, three?

I found that the only way I could truly dispose of anger was to deal with the root cause of why I was so angry. I was so resentful toward life that I harbored a deep anger for it. I didn't smile a lot and tried to avoid physical contact, such as hugging, whenever I could. I was angry and didn't know how to let it go until I dealt with the root of it. For me, right at the core of it all was bitterness.

The Bible is full of examples of how anger and bitterness made some people go astray from their walk with God. I think one of the most notable examples is Jonah. In this instance God used Jonah to minister to His people, however, when things didn't go as Jonah had hoped for, Jonah was never mentioned in the Bible again. After initially running from his assignment to go to the citizens of Nineveh to deliver a word from God, Jonah relented. The citizens repented and God had a change of heart, deciding not to punish His children for their disobedience. Jonah was upset and became bitter toward God because God decided to give His people another chance. In Jonah's mind, this made him look like a fool because God had not done to the people what His initial word said He would do.

Do you know any Jonahs in your life? People who tend to get mad at the world when things don't go their way? I do, and I don't even have to look far. I can simply stand in front of the mirror. Once upon a time I was Jonah.

Throughout this book you will constantly see examples of how I allowed bitterness to take root in my life. Even though I was in church being used by God, I wasn't reaping the benefits of being His servant. I constantly equated God to how man treated me. If I did something wrong, then I stopped praying to

Him. The spirit of shame would tell me I wasn't worthy enough to be in His presence, but God isn't man! God loves us throughout all of our faults. He was there with us when we messed up but yet He still stood with open arms waiting on us to come back to Him. He never left us nor has He ever forsaken us, however, bitterness can make one think otherwise.

Bitterness can be a deep root that is hard to identify. A person can go through their entire life not knowing that they are bitter. Once it rears its ugly head, they find themselves simply operating in life instead of living life.

In my opinion, I was doing everything that I was supposed to be doing in the eyes of the Lord. But I didn't see anything manifesting from it. I was still struggling financially and still feeling as though I was not living the blessed life that the Bible talked about. I couldn't understand why I wasn't living the good life on earth as it is in heaven. I mean I was paying my tithes, being faithful in the church, serving my man and woman of God the best way I knew how, but I wasn't seeing the fruit of my labor.

One day I was in church and all of a sudden I started crying. The more I tried to stop the tears from coming, the more I cried. Now I am not one to just be sitting up somewhere crying unless something has really upset me. On that particular day, though, nothing in my natural knowledge had me distressed.

So there I stood with my face and the front of my dress soaked from tears. God would have chosen a day that I had put on my pretty makeup to deal with me on an issue that I hadn't even known existed within. It was something that He was about to bring to the forefront of my life; not just bring it up, but also cleanse me of it. On that day He showed me that I had a huge root of bitterness and it came from dealing with life.

For the majority of my life I knew rejection. From being given up at birth to breakups with boyfriends and friends, I knew how it felt not to be wanted. Every time the topic of rejection was being ministered in church, I was the first one up at the altar getting prayed for. In my heart, though, I knew there was something else at the core keeping me from reaping the promises of God. However, not in a million years would I have guessed that rejection wasn't my most poisonous issue. Bitterness was, even though in all of this time it had not been visible to me.

On that day in church when my tears refused to subside, the man of God stood up and said, "For twenty-one of you, God is uprooting a deep root of bitterness."

Immediately I started screaming out in the spirit. I was one of the twenty-one people. But how did I become bitter? I had practiced forgiving the people who had hurt me. Heck, I could even carry on a good conversation with some of them. But on the same token, some people had done more hurtful things to me than others. I mean, how can I forgive someone that had hurt me so deeply that it caused my own walk to be hindered? It caused me to stand idle and cemented when I should have been running…chasing after God.

Too often people can get caught up in the tangle of lies and deceit that the world gives. It is no longer a happily ever after but it is *just-let-me-get-through-the-day-and-the-hour*. We start to take tolerance pills to help us tolerate more things instead of dealing with the real issues at hand. We find reasons as to why we are operating the way that we are instead of saying, "I need to find another way because this way isn't working and I need to break free from the chains that are binding me."

I speak from experience; I was a tolerance pill popping junky. I started tolerating life instead of living it. I found myself taking more and more tolerance pills just to get through the day. When I got saved I started reading my Bible and trying to put into practice what I was learning about kingdom living. Then life started happening.

Life had already started off on a bitter note for me. In the midst of me growing in my mother's womb, she made plans to give me away.

I made my debut on earth December 28, 1980. For many years I never looked at my birthday as being special. It was just another day. There weren't any parties because it was so close to Christmas day. I always heard the same tune that many who have a birthday around that time of year may hear. "Here is your Christmas and your birthday gift together." But of course the single gift was always wrapped in Christmas wrapping, which meant it wasn't really a birthday present at all. Up until just a couple years ago I never knew what it was like to actually celebrate my birth.

You see, from the age of eight, which is when my memory becomes less fuzzy and I can remember things, I felt alone. I didn't feel as though I belonged anywhere. By the age of nine, when the suicide attempts started, I felt like I was taking up space here on the earth and that no one really wanted me here. By the age of fifteen I had tried to kill myself the amount of times that totaled every year I'd been on earth.

I could be in a crowded room and still feel alone. I felt like I didn't have any purpose and constantly questioned why I was even born. It was a continuous battle with suicide up until the age of twenty-eight. The thoughts would come and linger, then ultimately I would entertain them. "I don't need to be here. No one would even miss me."

Over-the-counter pills were my preference in my suicide attempts because even though I didn't want to be here, I didn't want to endure any pain. I had already endured enough.

My first suicide attempt was at the age of nine. I went to the local grocery store and there I stole my first bottle of pills. I returned home to find my adoptive parents putting up a fan in my bedroom. I got some water, took half of the bottle and lay on the bed. The goal was that by the time they finished putting up the fan I would be dead or near death. So when I opened my eyes and found the fan installed and a cover had been placed over me, I started to cry. I buried my head into my covers and asked God why I was still here. I didn't want to be alive anymore. I was tired of feeling an internal loneliness. I wanted to feel the love that I had seen on television; the Huxtables, the Tanners and the Winslows. I looked at those television shows and took a mental picture of the type of family I wanted. Where was that kind of unconditional love and when would it be my turn at it?

Per Webster Dictionary, depression is defined as a state of feeling sad: a serious medical condition in which a person feels very sad, hopeless, and unimportant and often is unable to live in a normal way. I was a very depressed child from as far back as I can remember. Back then I didn't have a relationship with God nor did I try to form one. In my opinion, the state I was in was all His fault.

Before my tenth birthday I had been raped and survived a molestation so horrific it made me fearful of intimacy with men. Fear would grip my heart during intimacy and I could emotionally detach myself from the act. Just the idea of being left alone with another man would put me in fear. This used to drive my ex-boyfriends crazy. They would want to cuddle up and watch a movie, while I would periodically get up and make myself busy. Any signs of intimacy, even in the movies, would make me freeze up. I didn't even want to watch it, let alone participate in it.

As years went on I found myself emotionally detaching more and more from society. I was becoming a nervous, paranoid individual. I was constantly afraid of who was going to hurt me, who was going to talk about me, who would want me and who would reject me. The list would go on and on. I wondered if I would ever get to the point where I stopped looking at who didn't want me and only look toward the one who did.

The search for me.

I was in a program called Upward Bound. Upward Bound is a program that helps those children that excel in school and are potential first time college bound students. They would expose us to different cultures through restaurant experiences and field trips. On one of those trips I met someone who would help me fill in the missing blanks of questions that had been in my mind since the age of nine.

We were on the bus on our way to a field trip in Charleston, South Carolina. One of the chaperones sat across from me. She started talking to me and kept asking me who my parents were. I started catching an attitude and she apologized, saying she was only asking because I looked like someone she

11

knew. On one final attempt she asked me who my parents were. The image of the words that had been haunting me since I was nine came to my head. Suddenly, instead of giving her the name of my adoptive parents, I blurted out the name listed as my biological mother on the adoption papers. The woman jumped up and said, "I knew it. Girl, you look just like your momma."

I can't even express how excited I was to find someone who knew the woman who had given birth to me. I ended up spending the entire trip talking to the chaperone. She gave me the names of my aunts, my grandmother and great grandmother. I had gotten on that bus with blanks, but when I got back home I had some answers. I immediately grabbed the phone book and started calling every phone number of the names she had given me. I lucked up and ended up getting into contact with a couple of my siblings. Fifteen years old and I felt as though I was finally about to be the girl that had the happy ending.

It started out with a phone call every day, as we called each other at night or right after school. It was nice getting to know my brothers and sisters. Then I received the call that my birth mother wanted to make contact with me. I had never asked anyone to put me in contact with her. After all, I was the rotten lemon that she didn't want.

The older I got, I would revisit those adoption papers. My vocabulary grew as well as my understanding of what the papers meant. I knew I was unwanted and in my head I had fabricated my own reasons as to why. I wanted to avoid the truth by not hearing it from the horse's mouth.

My brother called me telling me that my birth mother wanted me to call her and if I didn't, she was going to contact Department of Social Services and tell them that I was reaching out to my biological family. Nine times out of ten, they would turn around and tell my adoptive parents, who knew nothing about what I was doing thus far.

Fear struck me. Growing up in foster care I often lived in fear of the social worker coming to get me. Even though I had been permanently adopted, a part of me always wondered if I'd have to pack my bags one day due to no longer being wanted.

Everything I had done as far as contacting my birth mother's family had been done in secret. I hadn't told my adoptive parents. Eventually I confessed to them what I was doing. My adoptive mother looked me dead in my eyes and said, "That's fine. We knew you would find out one day." The weight left me and joy took over.

I called my brother up, informing him that he could make the connection between my birth mother and me. I kept wondering how she would sound. How would she receive me? I was full of nerves. My nerves were put to rest when I was finally on the phone with her.

Initially it was just standard pleasantries. Finally she asked me the question that I had wanted to ask her but was afraid to.

"Have you ever wondered why I gave you up?"

I gave her the reasoning I'd used for self-comforting over the years. "I just felt as though you did it because you wanted me to have a better life than what you could provide. So I am okay with that."

"No, that's not it," she said. "I just didn't want you."

She might as well have taken a dull, rusted pocket knife and performed open heart surgery on me. Tears formed and began to spill from my eyes. She went on to say how she was so young at the time of her pregnancy and wasn't prepared to raise a child. The conversation was short after that point and I was left with, "Well, this is my number. You can use it if you want to," and then there was a click in my ear.

Both tears of relief and hurt fell. I was happy that I'd gotten the conversation over with, but hurt because the dream that I had dreamed all of those years had been crushed down to me simply being unwanted.

For the next several months I was in heaven. I was talking to my biological brother every day. Even though I had my birth mother's phone number, I didn't dial it. She had told me that she didn't want me and I felt as though I would be bothering her by calling her. My brother and I were very close and we shared everything. Up until that point we had only talked on the phone, so I was elated when I was invited to spend

15

the weekend with my family. I gained permission from my adoptive parents and off I went to meet that side of my life.

Meeting my birth mother for the first time, I was full of emotions. My first impression was that she was a very pleasant woman, even aiding me in meeting up with my other siblings that were both older and younger than me. Real blood family…a dream come true!

That weekend was perfect! The next day it was Sunday. During church I'd finally felt the pulling of the Holy Spirit, urging me to give my life to Christ; not because I'd been told to, but because I wanted to. I got saved that same summer day, and that Monday all HELL broke loose.

Apparently that Sunday after going up and getting saved my birth mother had told a lie on me. She started calling everyone with the lie. I was accused of something that I didn't do. Me and some of my family members started falling out. Immediately I thought, *Is this the saved life?*

My adoptive mother had received a phone call as well, and the next thing I knew I was being accused of all kinds of stuff. Lies and more lies came and the arguing grew and grew. I knew folks were lying on me, but the enemy had sent someone that knew how to tell a lie so well, one would have sworn it was the truth. Unfortunately my adoptive mother did believe the lie and my birth mother was encouraging it. I was so hurt by my adoptive mother's actions.

Later that Monday afternoon I heard a voice say, "Go and tell your adoptive mother that you forgive her." Ever since I had first gotten baptized at thirteen, I started hearing a voice in my head. It wasn't until later, after developing my walk with God, that I learned the voice was that of the Holy Spirit. It was just like in I Samuel 3:4.

That the LORD called Samuel: and he answered, Here am I.

I would hear His voice and on this day He was telling me to go and forgive.

A spirit of disobedience immediately fell upon me. I had all the reasons in the world why I shouldn't have to forgive anybody, but how people should be coming to apologize to me.

God wouldn't let me off the hook that easily, so finally I walked onto the front porch, where my adoptive mother sat, with my forgiveness speech in hand. I read it word for word from my heart.

I was in complete shock when my very own words of forgiveness were used against me. I found myself in a deeper mess than what I had been in before. I went back into my room, sat on my bed and was completely distraught…and confused.

"I did what you told me to do," I looked up to the heavens and said. "Do you see how it turned out?" At that point, I couldn't see how forgiving someone had benefited me at all. It was at that very moment that a root of bitterness started covering me and I didn't even know it at the time. It was the start of me making lemonade.

The unwanted events in life that I wish never happened. The things I wish I could turn back the hands of time and do over. And the unwanted parts of my past that I wish I never had to experience became the main things that made me realize I was wanted by the King Himself. God had a plan far greater

than I could have ever imagined.

     Letasha   was born on December 28, 1980 at Lexington County
Hospital.   We have no
information on the birth but believe it to be full term and normal.

Chapter Two What can be done with Rotten Lemons?

Step Two: Choosing the Right Lemons

It is important that you take the time to examine all of your lemons. You can have huge lemons with brown spots. Those lemons can't be used. Those type of lemons are about to spoil and you will not be able to extract a lot of juice from them.

As a little girl I would often find myself in my parents' backyard picking flowers, making a wish, and blowing as hard as I could to make all the petals fly away. My momma had told me that if after I made a wish all the petals were gone, then my wish was supposed to come true.

I remember many times praying just to be happy. It seemed that I was always sad and depressed; wondering what, if, when and why couldn't I just be happy. Many summer days were filled in that backyard with me picking flowers, closing my eyes, blowing and making wishes. It never failed that every time I opened my eyes I'd find that one or two petals had

20

refused to be blown away. As a grown woman I found myself in that place many times where everything had blown away, but one or two things remained lingering.

Why hadn't my wish come true?

Many times I found myself trying so hard to belong, only to realize that I didn't fit into the puzzle. I wasn't the missing piece to complete the pretty picture that I was trying to create. If you've ever put together a puzzle, then you know that the hardest part is the middle section. That's where we are constantly trying to fit random pieces together that we think should fit. We try and try however many times only to find that the piece doesn't fit into the place in which we are trying to make it fit. All that time wasted, time that we can never get back.

For the first part of my life I didn't know that I wasn't being raised by my natural family. However, at the age of nine was when I'd found my adoption papers. I wasn't at a point where I could understand everything, but key words like 'adoption' and 'birth mother' I recognized. For the first time I saw the name of my birth mother but I didn't know what it all meant until one family gathering.

Several family members were present. We all sat around the table enjoying Sunday's dinner. Afterward my cousins and I were playing outside. One of my boy cousins was talking to another cousin. I went over wanting to be a part of the conversation and I was rejected, being told that blood was thicker than water. The cousins turned around and left me standing there alone.

I went off crying and my daddy found me asking me what was wrong. I told him what was said to me. He was speechless, but the look of hurt in his eyes spoke volumes. He simply turned around and walked away. I had been able to put two and two together; the cousins' words and the words on the adoption papers. This became something that began to haunt me. Even though the foster home that I started out in eventually became my adoptive family, the words foster child became a tagline associated with my name. "Here is Tasha the first foster child. Tasha was the first one that we got." By the age of thirteen I stopped looking at myself as being an adopted child, and instead saw myself as a foster child. It was like a constant pounding hammer to my head that translated to, "You don't belong."

Growing up, the only man I had ever known as a father was my adoptive father, but our relationship wasn't a close one. I loved him, but that constant reminder that blood was thicker than water always separated us. My father was a great man and as a child he always made sure we had food and a place to stay. But because of others, my establishing a true father-daughter relationship with him was nearly impossible.

I had always felt a need to find out who my biological parents were. I was looking for validation that in my natural mindset only they could give. Up until I did get in touch with my birth mother, I had spent what felt like a lifetime looking for her or my birth father to come through the door and say, "You are my daughter and I want you back." As a foster child my entire desire was to gain a true family; one that I could call my own. I loved my adoptive family but part of me always felt like I was missing something.

Why doesn't anyone love me? Finding part of me.

I was looking for love in all the wrong places. I'm sure you've heard that line before. Love is an emotion that over the years some people has truly taken out of context. Love is more than a feeling, it is more than sex and it is more than two people being together. Love is an action. Love is a verb, so that means that action has to be behind it. There has to be more to it than just saying, "I love you." A person's actions have to meet the words out of their mouth. Not to beat a dead horse into the ground, but one's actions have to mimic the word.

For God so loved the world, that he gave his only begotten Son. (John 3:16)

There are two types of love I want to address. Phileo love which is based off emotions; you scratch my back and I'll scratch yours. You will find this type of love in friendships. Then there is Agape Love. Agape love is a love that will love you regardless of what you say or do. Agape love is what Jesus showed the world. Through Jesus' death, He brought us back into the original covenant of God.

In my opinion, my adoptive family could not demonstrate that Agape love. I always wanted to be a daddy's girl. I got in the way of that by feeling that I couldn't be my adoptive father's because we weren't related by blood. He wasn't my real daddy. The only ones who could possibly give me the love I sought was my biological family.

I once had hope that my birth family would be that signing factor that I sought. The ones that would shower me with the love and acceptance that I wanted. I enjoyed having my brother in my life, but I would look at my friends who had their fathers in their lives. I listened to their stories of how they could call and talk to their dads about anything, or stories of what their fathers did for them. A part of me would get envious. They had something that I wanted so badly.

A father.

The word 'Father' appears 1,126 times in the Bible. It was very important that God not only identified Himself as

25

God, but as a Father also. God created both male and female to have dominion over the earth. This can be confirmed in Genesis 1:26. A father is one who has begotten a child, so of course God was the ultimate Father. However, many people look toward their natural father for definition and validation of who they are in life.

My birth mother didn't want me but what about my father?

In January 2003, there I was standing in a hallway of my college apartment. I was in perfect view of the entrance of the doorway. I stood with butterflies in my stomach. The man who I was told could possibly be my father entered the building. Fear leaped inside of me with a huge amount of joy and relief. He immediately began walking straight toward me full blast. It wasn't a slow, tentative walk with a pause, as if he was hesitant about the situation before him. In fact, it was just the opposite. It was almost as if he was excited. In return, excitement leaped all through my being. With each step he took toward me I began imagining what his first words would be to me; after he pulled me in for a hug and wrapped me tightly in his arms of course.

"My baby. I wouldn't have left you had I known," is what I imagined him saying. *"I am so glad that you found me and now we can build from here on out."*

Once he approached me he didn't exactly pull me in for that hug. Instead he reached out for my hand. I looked down at his extended hand. No, it wasn't a hug, but it was a start, a good start I thought. I placed my hand inside of his and smiled. There was still a chance he could want my hand in order to pull me in for that hug I had envisioned. With only positive thoughts, my soul rejoiced.

"Hi," he said. "I don't think you are mine." Cut to the chase, point blank. No feelings involved whatsoever. Stoic. Cold.

After that, everything else he said to me was a blur. His initial words cut a part of me that I never thought could hurt. That part that I kept at bay in order to protect. That part that I kept a wall around. But this man had caught me in a vulnerable state where I had let my guards down. I had experienced hurt before, but not hurt like this.

I snapped out of my daze to him asking me for my birth mother's phone number. He pulled out his cell phone and I rambled her number off to him. He called her and talked with her for a couple minutes. After that, he ended the call, said good-bye to me, and walked out of the same door that he had come. That was it. No, "Let's get a DNA test," or anything.

I just stood there for what seemed like hours, replaying the incident over and over in my head. *He doesn't want me. He doesn't want me,* was all I could think to myself. After so long, I eventually turned around to go upstairs to my room. With each step I took up those stairs, all I kept saying to myself was, "Why doesn't anyone want me?"

Once in my room I buried myself in my sheets to cry in my tears of shame. It was after that when I started looking for that father figure that seemed like it was never going to find me. I was going to be a daddy's girl if it was the last thing I did.

I was so consumed with the hurt from the meeting with my prospective father; it ignited me having yet another case against God. God was supposed to give me my heart's desires. I desired nothing more than to have my biological father in my life. That dream had just gone out the window. Not only had my hopes been abandoned in that hallway, but I felt abandoned by God as well.

I couldn't understand any of it. I wasn't a bad person. I tried to be nice to people, so why did these things keep happening to me? I deserved better. So of course with that feeling came a sense of entitlement as well.

Per Webster Dictionary, entitlement is the fact of having a right to something; the amount to which a person has a right; the belief that one is inherently deserving of privileges or special treatments. I felt that because I had given my life to God that I deserved to have everything I wanted. That was one of the biggest mistakes in my Christian walk that I could have ever made. I had a hidden motive behind the reason I served God, and when I didn't get what I wanted, I became more and bitterer.

I was just like Hannah in I Samuel of the Bible. Hannah had to watch as her husband's second wife, Peninnah, gave birth, while year after year Hannah bared no children. Every year Hannah grew more and more bitter. In those times a woman was not deemed to be a good wife if she couldn't give her husband any children. So can you imagine how she felt to not only be the first wife of Elkanah, but to sit back and watch another woman do what she couldn't?

She laid on the altar crying, her lips moving, but no words coming out. She might have looked like a crazy woman to some, but she was so consumed with her petition to God that she was unaware of who was watching. Then, according to I Samuel 1:14:

Eli said unto her, How long wilt thou be drunken? Put away thy wine from thee.

It was at that point her heart grew heavy. She wanted a child, and she didn't want to go another year without having what she felt entitled to.

I Samuel 1: 9-11 reads: *⁹So Hannah rose up after they had eaten in Shiloh, and after they had drunk. Now Eli the priest sat upon a seat by a post of the temple of the LORD.¹⁰ And she was in bitterness of soul, and prayed unto the LORD, and wept sore. ¹¹ And she vowed a vow, and said, O LORD of hosts, if thou wilt indeed look on the affliction of thine handmaid, and remember me, and not forget thine handmaid, but wilt give unto thine handmaid a man child, then I will give him unto the LORD all the days of his life, and there shall no razor come upon his head.*

In verse 10 you read where it states Hannah was bitter in her soul. She was afflicted in her mind and in her body about what she thought she should have. Finally she said, "I will give him back to you, God." It was at that moment she realized that what she wanted so badly (a baby), she would have to give back to God as a sacrifice.

When I was searching for my birth father I was walking in the spirit of entitlement. I said, "God I want this. I deserve this." But I didn't deserve it. God tests our motives about why we pray for the things we pray for. He wants to see if that thing will be a god to us. This sounds strange, right? I mean why would He not want to give us what we desire when His Word says otherwise?

God doesn't want to withhold anything back from us. Many times we put ourselves in places that hurt us more than help us. We don't put ourselves in a place of constant sacrifice where we don't feel entitled to anything. We love to sing songs saying we can't live without Him and how He is our everything. If that is true, then why is it so hard to trust Him when things don't go our way? I am looking in the mirror at this one. I can't afford to look around the walls or down the aisle because that was me. I clapped my hands, told people about this benevolent God that I didn't truly believe myself. Instead of looking at the treasures that God had given me, I stayed focused on what I felt like He wasn't giving me.

I was born to a woman who didn't want me. Per the notes in the medical file, there weren't any signs of prenatal care. Instead of saying, "Thank you, God, for not allowing her to abort me," I said, "Why didn't she want me?" Some of the things I went through as a child such as being raped and molested, I'd ask God why He allowed those things to happen to me. Instead of telling Him how it was His fault that this person and that person hurt me, I should have been thanking Him that I was still in my right mind. "Thank you, Lord, that I know right from wrong. Thank you, Lord, for putting me in a place that regardless of what is happening to me, I know that I don't have to hurt anyone else the way I was hurt."

It is always easier to see the negative things in life, but when we start seeing how God has truly protected us and allowed us to continue to walk on this earth in our right mind, it should make us feel grateful. However, at that time in my life I hadn't gotten to that point yet. I was still stuck on the brown spots in life.

Chapter Three
Rolling out of Order

Step Three: Time for a Washing

Once you have separated the bad from the good lemons, wash off the lemons you will use. You now want to give them a good roll back and forth on a sanitize surface. This will help you when it comes to juicing them. It gets the juices to start flowing inside the lemons. After that, cut them in half and start juicing each lemon half.

I thought my problems would be solved once I'd found my birth family. I had looked for them for years. I wanted to find that acceptance that, in my eyes, being part of a bonded by blood family would enable. It would validate me. I was not winning that side of the battle in my eyes. I had graduated high school and was in my first year of college. After meeting with some members of my birth family, I still didn't fill as though the void had been filled. It seemed as though nothing would ever be right, but that changed on November 17, 1999.

It was during my first semester of college that I became part of the statistics. I was trying to go to sleep one night but I was having stomach issues. I could not sleep on my stomach, which was unusual because that was how I normally slept. I went to the Student Services and told the nurse what I was experiencing. She outright asked me if there was a possibility that I could be pregnant. Even though I denied such, she went on and tested me anyway, using the line, "Just to be on the safe side."

I remember laying there on the examination table when the nurse came back in. She said the words, "You're pregnant." Ironically, and to my own surprise, all of a sudden that fear that I once had turned to joy. As much as I was not ready for a child in my life, I would now have a purpose in life. And I was going to make sure that I was able to provide for my child.

I started going to extreme measures in preparing for the birth of my baby. I signed up for housing and began looking for a better paying job than the local restaurant I worked at whenever I was back at home. I knew that it was not going to be easy, but I was going to try to raise my child to the best of my ability. I didn't have much faith in the baby's father. We weren't in a relationship so I knew I had to make the plans to raise this baby by myself. So I laid out my game plan and that next week I went home to break the news to my family.

My goal was to tell my sister because I knew that she would tell my momma, sparing me the task. I felt better with the news going through my sister because by the time my momma found out, I would be back at school. I broke the news in a very creative way. I asked for the rocking chair that I'd bought for my sister when she was pregnant with my niece. When she asked me why I needed it, I told her about my own pregnancy. Needless to say, she was shocked.

I went back to school with joy in my heart because I was about to have a baby. All I could think about was the love a baby could give me and how I was going to be accepted, and most importantly, I was going to be loved. I knew one thing for certain and two things for sure; I was having a baby and no way would it reject me.

I was on the go preparing for the birth of my baby. I went to the city housing department and signed up for low-income housing. Since the apartment I'd been staying in was part of school housing, I knew I wouldn't have been able to stay there after having the baby.

On December 3, 1999 I woke up that morning and found myself sleeping on my stomach. I felt in my spirit that something was wrong and I started crying. My roommate consoled me by telling me that I was overreacting, so I ended up not even bothering to call my doctor. My scheduled appointment was only a couple days away anyhow.

On December 5, 1999 I went to the doctor's office and was told that I was four months along. As my doctor examined me, I noticed a concerned look on her face. When I questioned her she replied that she couldn't find the baby's heartbeat. I instantly went into panic mode. She calmed me down by telling me it was okay; with me being that early in the pregnancy, it was normal. She assured me that on my next visit she would try again, and if at that point the heartbeat couldn't be found, then that would be cause for alarm.

I accepted her reasoning, but it still didn't sit well with me. But she was the professional so I took her word for it and didn't press the issue.

I went home for Christmas break and by then my momma had found out about my pregnancy. Needless to say, she was not happy. She was so upset that I had gone off to college and gotten pregnant. Even though she and I didn't get along when I was growing up, our relationship was bittersweet. I have learned to forgive and move on and we have a better relationship now, but back then was a totally different story. After she read me the riot act, my concerns went back to that of the health of my baby. I called the local doctor and made an appointment for December 20th.

I still had hope.

With no transportation to the doctor's office, even though it was on the other side of town, I started walking. One of my friends rode by and picked me up and took me the rest of the way. She dropped me off and I went inside. Once I arrived the doctor ran some tests and asked if I could get a ride to the main hospital so that I could have an ultrasound performed. I told her that I could possibly get one the following day, but not right then and there. I'd been lucky enough to get a ride to that appointment.

I told her that I would call her back once I could confirm a ride, and then I walked home. I called everyone who I knew that had a car. One of my friends, who was pregnant herself, offered to take me once her boyfriend got off work, so the appointment was made for the next evening.

The next day I got my ultrasound done. They informed me that I could call my doctor's office the following day for the results. In the car, on my way home, eeriness came over me and I could not stop crying. I was like that for the entire night.

By morning I was filled with so much anxiety that I was not going to wait on the doctor to tell me anything. I called her at 9:05 a.m. When I talked to the nurse to ask her about my results she asked if I could get someone to bring me back down to the office.

A sheet of dread covered me. I could only think the worst as I started yelling and screaming, "My baby is dead! Oh, my God, my baby dead!" The nurse kept telling me to calm down, but I wouldn't hear of it. Realizing that getting me to calm down was out of the question, she was forced to further inform me of the worst.

She proceeded to tell me that according to the ultrasound, my baby had, in fact, been dead for a couple of weeks. She warned that if I didn't act fast in having the baby removed from my womb, toxins would be released in my body that could harm or kill me. That was on December 22nd. I remember crying and begging the nurse if I could just have one more day with my baby inside of me. Please don't think it's weird or strange. Okay, maybe from the outside looking in it was, but my baby had been my hope; the one person that was going to fill the void I'd been missing all of my life. Didn't I deserve to have one more day of hope?

My appointment was scheduled for the next day. When I hung up the phone all I could do was continue to wail about how my baby was dead. My momma heard me and she came in the room and tried to comfort me. I shrugged her off of me and said, "Isn't this what you wanted? You didn't want me pregnant." I got up, put on my work uniform and stormed out of the house. I had been working at the same local restaurant since I was in high school. I had already made arrangements before I left school to work when I was home for Christmas break.

Walking to work seemed like the longest walk ever. There were tears streaming down my eyes with a hurting heart and the only thing I could think about was that I needed to get to work. I excelled at work and school, so often when things were going wrong in life, I would fall head first into one of those areas, only submerging when I thought I had overcome whatever issue I was going through.

I didn't know how to deal with stuff at that time. The only thing I knew was to work and go to school. I went to work, crying the entire time. One of my coworkers, who was also pregnant, kept asking me what my baby's name was going to be. I simply answered her, not wanting to go into details about how I'd miscarried. I had no clue that she was trying to be funny, that she knew all along that I had lost my baby. One our mutual friends had shared it with her. That was her sick way of trying to get me to come out and say it. I was so distraught that I wasn't in tune with anything that was going on around me.

On December 23rd I ended up having a procedure called a D&C. The day after the procedure I had to go to the doctor to make sure there were no after effects of the procedure. The doctor took an ultrasound and I remember asking if I could have a picture. I knew that nothing was there, but I just wanted something because I didn't have anything else to remember my baby by. I wanted that picture even though it was a sign of what could have been instead of what it was…or what I wanted it to be.

Needless to say, Christmas was not that good for me. I was in pain from the D&C, so I stayed off work a couple days. When I went back to work, that same coworker was at it again, questioning me about what I was going to name my baby. I flipped out! I was slicing tomatoes at the time. I remember holding the knife in one hand and shaking so badly that the cutting board fell onto the floor. The manager had to pry the knife out of my hand, afterward ordering me to go take a break. I went to the break room and needless to say my coworker never asked me that question again.

Looking back on the incident, I think it's safe to say that I might have been going through something similar to post-partum depression. I had hit a brown spot in my life and I didn't know how to overcome it, but I had my ways of trying.

I was a dreamer, literally. Once I fell into a deep sleep, it was inevitable that I would have a dream. On my birthday I prayed to God, asking Him if I could just have one dream of me holding my baby in my arms. I believed in my heart that would give me peace. The next morning I woke up and saw the sunlight and immediately started crying, because for the first time in a long time, I hadn't had a dream. I felt as though God had betrayed me.

I continued the process of getting up every morning, going to work and getting off. I had to walk across a bridge on my way to and from work. One day I just stood there for about thirty minutes contemplating whether or not I would jump. I realized that the bridge wasn't high enough to kill me, just break some bones, so I continued my walk home crying with every step.

That was over ten years ago, but I still find myself getting emotional about the miscarriage. Before the D&C was done they did a final ultrasound, in which I was informed the baby was a girl. I still find myself looking at other kids that are the age my daughter would have been, wondering what type of parent I would have been and what kind of child she would have been. How did I get to that point where all my hopes and dreams laid within one child?

Questions:

1.   Are you still holding on to a painful memory?

2.   What are you gaining by holding on to that memory? How has it made your life better?

3.   Is God getting the glory from what you are holding on to?

Everything had gone astray in my life after the loss of my baby, not that it was in any type of order before. This was not the good life that I was told I would live once I got saved. It seemed to me that my life was full of hurt and pain. And the choir kept singing the same song: "Why me?"

Too often I found myself wanting to concentrate on the brown spots in life, the spots of rejection, abandonment and loneliness. These were the things that could not add to my life. Still, I wanted to stay stuck there because I thought I deserved every bad thing that happened to me. I continued making cases against God and growing bitterer. I would constantly look at the clock and wish I could turn back the hands of time; wishing I could change certain situations and life issues.

Life happens every day regardless if we want it to or not. Time stops for no one and we can get stuck in the brown spots in life or we can discard those brown spots and move on.

Losing my child was one of the hardest brown spots that I had to get over. For the next several years I would routinely go into a depression every December. In fact, I never celebrated my birthday until 2007. That was the first time I woke up on my birthday and was actually happy and wanted to celebrate. I can't put my finger on a single thing that triggered the emotion. All I know is that I woke up smiling and I felt like I had a purpose for living.

All things work together for the good of those who love the Lord. (Romans 8:28)

I was lost in a sea of hurt and despair. I didn't want to move. I didn't want help. When I lost my child I felt like a failure. People would say to me, "God doesn't put anything on you that you can't bear." They would say, "God knows all and you don't know what would have happened with that baby." The worst thing that I think anyone told me was, "Nothing happens unless God allows it. It must not have been in His will for you to have that child."

People often think they are saying things that will comfort a person when something as simple as a hug could go a long way. I was depressed and I wanted my baby, so to hear that God didn't want to give me my child only intensified my anger toward God.

One night while in my room I couldn't go to sleep. I sat there staring at the ceiling of my apartment with my hands rested on my stomach. Then I heard the Holy Spirit whisper, "It's not your fault."

I immediately knew in my heart what God was referring to. It had been over twelve years since I'd lost my first child and my heart still had a bitter root towards God. It was as though a deep sleep came over me and I went back to that time in my life when I was pregnant. I was so stressed out, nineteen and pregnant and a freshman in college. I felt that I had let everyone down that believed in me.

I didn't have enough money to attend the college of my choice, which was out of state, so I made plans to stay in my hometown and attend a community college. My high school teacher offered to take time out of her day to drive me to different colleges. I gladly accepted her offer. When I got in my high school teacher's car, she had college applications, a clipboard and a pen.

"Fill these out. We are going to these colleges and talk to the admission department," she informed me. She got me into college and I dropped the ball by getting pregnant not even a month into my first semester. Having to call her and tell her I was pregnant was such a heavy burden. She didn't get mad though, she simply said, "Well, now you will have two people proud of you when you get your degree…your child and me."

The guilt I had for having wasted her time wore heavy on me. Then there had been the process of trying to find a place to stay with a baby, a better job, and the list went on. Perhaps ultimately the baby could not live in a stressed environment, which was why I miscarried. It was only natural that I would have blamed myself. But when the Holy Spirit told me that it wasn't my fault, I believed Him.

In 2001 I went down the same path after being physically attached while 5 months pregnant. I went into premature labor and I had a stillborn baby boy. I have two angels in heaven that hold a part of my heart. I loved my babies from the moment I was told about them. I had already planned their future without having heard their first cry. People would ask me why I was crying for babies I never even had and got to form a relationship with here on earth. My reason was simple. I told them that I cried for those who I love.

This pain has now turned into a ministry. Since 2013 God has put me in the path of many people who have lost their child. Because of what I went through, I was able to talk to them and help them understand that it was okay to be sad. They had lost a part of themselves, but they shouldn't give up hope.

One of my most notable experiences to this day was when I was in the hair salon and this pregnant lady sat beside me. She and I started conversing and she began complaining about her pregnancy. I turned to her and I started telling her about how I carried my last baby until my fifth month and then something went wrong. I had a natural labor, water broke, contractions, and I had to push, but my baby was born lifeless. After telling her how even though my baby was in heaven, I wouldn't have traded the cravings, morning sickness or anything. She looked at me in tears and thanked me for reminding her that she was carrying a blessing. One of my toughest brown spots now gets glory for God!

Chapter Four:
The Things I hated BUT GOD

After several hours, she finally decided to place the youngest child (born December 28) in foster care.

Step Four: Adding Sugar

Now that you have your lemon juice, you want to pour it in the pitcher. After doing so, pour one and a half cups of sugar into the pitcher. Fill the pitcher with the desired amount of water and then stir until all parts are combined.

When I was in college I had written a five-page paper on the things that I liked about myself. There were only two things on the list. However, I was also instructed to write down the things that I hated about myself. That list was very long. I literally hated myself. I could not stand to look in the mirror at the person staring back at me. I could not stand to be left in a room alone with myself. I couldn't stomach the sound of my own voice. I did not think that I was worthy enough to speak into my own life. I had such a low self-esteem issue that last year was my first time I actually looked in the mirror and could confess to myself that I was beautiful.

For years I would walk around with my head down, scared to look in the face of people because I did not want them to see me. I thought that I was ugly. People would say to me, "Stop walking with your head down. You can't see where you are going." Even though that was true, part of me didn't care where I was going. I had concluded that I wasn't destined to go anywhere anyhow.

You see, it was years of me believing that I had brought on everything bad that had happened to me. As a result of the rape and molestation, I felt that sex was the only way to get a man to want me. My only value was what was between my legs.

I am not ashamed to say it, but for the longest time I never even thought about getting married. My goal was a live-in boyfriend. I thought that as long as I had a live-in boyfriend, then that was all that I needed. I didn't need anything else because I was not going to be able to get anything else. That is what years of believing the sexual abuse was my fault had done to me. It made me think that I was not worthy of anything, and that I better accept whatever I had because that was the best I was going to get. Well I am here to tell you, screaming it at the top of my lungs, "The Devil is a Liar!"

It was God's intention for us to have the best of everything. In Genesis 1:26 it is stated that God created man in His image. In Psalms 139:14 it reads:

You are fearfully and wonderfully made.

In Deuteronomy 28:13 it reads:

You are the head and not the tail, above and not beneath.

The list goes on and on, however, when I was in the world, no one shared these things with me. Instead I was told, "You are ugly, you're too fat, your lips are not big enough, and your teeth are too big." Then I went in the church believing what had been instilled in me, unwilling to change because I had allowed the world to identify me.

My pastor, Bishop Theotis White, made a powerful statement one morning in Morning Glory, known as Sunday school. He said, "We readily accept the world's view, and readily reject God's Word." He read Matthew 24:35, which states:

Heaven and earth will pass away, but My words will by no means pass away.

I know that we are living in the last days. I have heard enough messages preached to know that. But the last time I checked, I was still standing on earth. Heaven is still standing. So guess what? God's Word is still reigning true.

We have to break out of the mindset that the world has put us in. The world has put us in a box. The world tells us that if we weigh over a certain amount of pounds, then we are too fat. That if we don't look a certain way, then we are not attractive. Every time God created something in Genesis 1 He stated that *"It was good."* God created me so therefore I am good. If I am good, then guess what? I am the only one that can allow someone to make me feel inferior, bad…like I'm a brown spot. That's right; all that time I had been giving the devil too much credit. God gave me the power to walk over scorpions and not be harmed. He also gave me the power to cast down any vain imagination that will exalt itself over Him. In other words, as much as I'd like to blame the devil for standing in my way to greatness, I was my worst enemy.

Nothing has power over us unless we hand over that power. When we release our power, we give that thing a right to dominate us. When we start standing in the authoritative power that God has given us, we stop allowing ourselves to be someone's garbage can. Yes, I said garbage can. If we allow people to dump things into our spirit that do not line up with what God has already said about us, then we are being a garbage can. Isn't that where you put the stuff that is no longer any good to you? We have to stop allowing people to put their point of views in our head and allowing that to be our god. God's Word is true. He is not going to say that you are fearfully and wonderfully made, then turn around and say that you are ugly or that you are fat. That is not the God I serve.

Let me clarify something. I am not saying that it is okay to be so big that it is unhealthy, because in John 10:10 it reads:

That I came so that you can have life and have it more abundantly

Those are the words of Christ Himself. So you cannot have that if you are unhealthy to the point where you cannot enjoy life. For the longest, we as a people, especially women, have become accustomed to saying what we don't have or what we are lacking in. But when we begin to embrace ourselves and start seeing ourselves as the beautiful creatures that God has created, then those negative mindsets will have no room to stand.

After dealing with a heart of bitterness for so long, I was consumed and could not see myself how God sees me. I had to take the Word of God and make the sweetness of His Word make the bitterness go away. I couldn't see my worth because my spirit was filled with the views of the world and how they saw me. God's Word started to erase those parts of me that I hated and started bringing life back into me.

This quiz below was designed to help you evaluate where you are at in life. Sometimes we can do something out of habit and not realize that it was not a good habit. It's not good for us to spend all of our time trying and please everyone else. We have to take time for ourselves. Taking the time to treat yourself and take care of yourself will help you build yourself up, and it will also help you develop in other areas of your life.

Self-Evaluation Moment:

1.   In the last few months, have you ever allowed your friends to make you feel inferior to them? I said allowed because no one can make you do anything, you have to allow them to do it. And if so, how many times?

2.   Do you love yourself?

3.   When was the last time you accepted a gift from someone without the thought they wanted something in return?

4.   After reading this chapter do you see where your aim was to please people and not God?

In the last three months have you put plans for yourself on the back burner in order to do something for someone else? If so, how many times?

The father of Letasha is unknown. Ms. ● does not seem to know who her (Letasha) father is.

Step Five: Test Tasting Time

Now that the lemon juice, water and sugar have all been stirred together, get a cup and taste a little bit. Depending on your taste buds, you may have to add more sugar or water to get it to the desired consistency. Once you are satisfied with the taste, you now have LEMONADE!

I was twenty-six years old when I decided to come to terms with some of the things that had happened to me, such as the rape, the molestation and years of rejection. The longer I waited, the harder it became for me to understand what was going on. I couldn't understand why I was in the church praising God and paying my tithes, but going home hurting. Why I felt like there was still part of me that I could not come to terms with. I can recall that it was on a Wednesday night when I found my answer.

Minster, now Elder Ella Gardner, was the speaker for the night and her topic was "Forgiveness is For You, Not For the Other Person." Through her spoken words, I realized that my heart had lacked forgiveness. I started working on forgiving those who had hurt me. I made a list of everyone who I was angry with and started writing out what they had done to me and how it affected me. After acknowledging what they did and going through how it affected me, I then asked God to remove the emotions that were attached to each situation. I asked God to cleanse my heart and my mind from those emotional scars and to fill those areas with His love; the love to forgive in spite of. Forgiveness was one of the key factors in releasing the lies that the world had told me; the things that I had allowed to consumed me instead of the Word of God.

I carried around so much stuff from my past as well as thoughts of what other people thought and felt about me. I had it all in my head and I believed it and lived it every day. Some of the things that happened to me in my past left me scarred. But guess what? Just like any physical scar, I knew my mental scars would heal as well. I just needed the right tools that would help me get beyond what had happen in order for healing to take place.

In the physical realm when we break our skin it starts to bleed. That is the first sign that we have been hurt. After we realize that we are bleeding, we go and rinse off the injured area and inspect it. We try to determine if it is something that we can deal with on our own, or if we will need to go to the doctor to get stitches. It is the same procedure when we are hurting internally as well.

You have to first realize that you are hurting. Then you have to analyze things to determine what is causing the pain. Some things you will have to deal with on your own, because it will be up to you to decide what you are willing to get over. For instance, in the middle of 2007 I fought a tough battle of alcoholism. Even at the age of fifteen I was an undercover alcoholic. I would find myself trying to drink my problems away. I slowed down through the years and learned not to abuse it. I felt like I had control over my drinking for almost three years. Then one day I was drinking a glass of water and it tasted like liquor sliding down my throat. Thank God that I had been prayed up. Had I not been, I probably would have gone on the hunt for the real thing and ruined my progress. I knew the Word of God and I had to stand on that. In that case that was me showing myself that I did not have to turn to liquor to feel better. All I had to do was look unto the hill from which comes my help. But I also had to get prayed for and delivered from it.

We cannot leave a cut unattended. We have to make sure no dirt gets into it, causing an infection. When you are being healed you have to make sure you are in the right environment. You have to get around people who can see where you are going, so when your foot wants to get weak they will help you stand. One must surround themselves with true, genuine friends.

There are two types of friends and I am going to go to scripture to explain them both. In the book of Matthew there are two cripple people. One sat at the gates of Beautiful and the other was brought through the roof and laid at the feet of Jesus for his healing. The one that sat at the gates of Beautiful friends brought him there every day. You will have friends that will help you stay in your mess and not help you out of it. They are the ones who will not be able to see you beyond where you are currently at, and they will be the ones chanting in your ear, "That is good. You better stay right there (in all of your mess)." Then you will have friends that will be like the ones who took the roof off. They saw their friend's future and they were not going to let it slip past them. They are the ones who will say, "You can get better. You can make it." Those are the friends who you need to hold onto.

This is the end of this book but only the beginning of the walk into a new life. Life can be very bitter but you have to have the right ingredients to turn a bitter thing into something sweet. When I learned how to forgive I began to become free.

You see, in my eyes before I really started trusting God I thought that my freedom would be in finding my biological family. I thought all my problems would be solved. God had given me great aunts, uncles, sisters and brothers, but I wanted my blood parents, the ones that had given me up. I thought my life could be reversed some if they would just take me back.

I remember one of my friends pulling me to the side and saying, "Tasha, what you have been searching for has been right in front of you all along." I couldn't believe her because she had both her biological parents. Then Jesus sent an angel by the name of Overseer Constance White who gave me the following scripture to study:

"Who owe their birth neither to bloods nor to the will of the flesh [That of physical impulse] nor to the will of man [that of a natural father] but to God. [They are born of God]. (John 1: 13 AMP)

I may not have been the will of my parents, but I am the will of my FATHER! He loves me with an unconditional love and He has a great and mighty plan for my life. Once that scripture really got into my system, slowly but surely, and with every tear that flowed, a deep root of bitterness was released from me. I remember going around trying to tell people how I was feeling and couldn't stop giggling because it was awkward for me. This is the joy and the peace that the Bible was talking about and, at last, I had felt it!

My countenance has changed and I not only feel it, but I am free. I wouldn't change this journey or this feeling for anything in the world. Forgiveness was and is the key that started unlocking the doors to my freedom. Once I truly forgave myself and those who I felt had hurt me or let me down, God started uprooting stuff and now I can say I don't want to look back. All I want to do is look forward and use my testimony of how I used to be to tell someone that there is a better way and they don't have to be bitter about life's circumstances. What may start off as bitter can be made to be sweet…with the right ingredients.

I affirmatively state that I am not the father of the child named above. I agree that since I am not the father of this child the Department of Social Services may place this child for adoption without further or additional permission from me. I also agree that I am waiving my right to be made a party to any future lawsuit involving adoption of this child, and I do not intend to participate in such a hearing.

On June 8, 1982 Ms. ⬤signed consent and waiver and requested that the Robinson's be allowed to adopt Letasha.

To Contact the Author, Please Write:

LeTasha S. Robinson
PO Box 15
Lexington, SC 29071

Email: Lsrobins@yahoo.com

Facebook: L. Robinson the Author
Twitter: Lsrobinson
Instagram: Lsrobins

www.ingramcontent.com/pod-product-compliance
Lightning Source LLC
Chambersburg PA
CBHW060423050426
42449CB00009B/2107